Promenades
AND
OTHER VERSE

by
Jessie Dismorr

FORGOTTEN POETS

Editor | Dick Whyte   Number 21 | 2024

JESSIE DISMORR (1885-1939) was born in Gravesend in Kent, and moved to Hampstead in the 1890s with her parents and four sisters. She attended the Slade School of Art (1902-1903), trained with Max Bohm at Étaples (1904), and later with Jean Metzinger at the Academie de La Palette in Paris (1910-1913), where she shared a studio with close friend and fellow artist Marguerite Thompson. In 1911-1912 she published her first abstract drawings in the avant-garde magazine *Rhythm*, and exhibited her paintings alongside the English Fauvists. Dismorr met Wyndham Lewis in 1913 and was a member of the Vorticist group, contributing illustrations to the first issue of *Blast* in 1914, and numerous poems to the second issue in 1915. Dismorr would go on to hand-write a small book of verse for John & Marguerite Storrs in 1918, some of which were published alongside new verses in *The Little Review* in 1919, about which John Rodker would write: "As far as I am concerned, Dismorr is one of the most important contributors to *The Little Review* today and four lines of her work outweigh the effusions of most others." She continued to paint and exhibit throughout the 1920s-30s, before sadly taking her own life in 1939, due to ongoing struggles with mental-health.

Publication Credits: selected verses from *Blast #2* (July 1915); *Poems* (self-published, 1918); & *The Little Review* (Aug. 1919). Quotations from Dismorr's essay 'Critical Suggestions', in *The Little Review* (Sep. 1919).

Cover: Dismorr – 'The Engine' & 'Design' (*Blast #2*, July 1915). Inside: Dismorr, et al. – various illustrations & ornaments (*Blast*, 1914-1915); Dismorr – 'Conversation' (*Tyro #2*, 1922); 'Izidora', 'Fergusson', 'Drawing', 'Study', & various ornaments (*Rhythm*, Summer 1911, Autumn 1911, Spring 1912), etc.

FORGOTTEN PRESS
Aotearoa | New Zealand

ISBN: 978-1-991310-14-9 (paperback) • 978-1-991310-15-6 (hardback)
978-1-991310-16-3 (ebook)

JESSIE DISMORR
PROMENADES & OTHER VERSE

BLAST

A selection of verses originally published
in *Blast* (1915).

POEMS

A selection of verses from the handwritten
collection, *Poems* (1918).

PROMENADES

A selection of verses originally published
in *The Little Review* (1919).

FORGOTTEN POETS

edited by **Dick Whyte**.

Missing Meters! Lost Lyrics! Vanished Verses!

LEWIS ALEXANDER
PEARL ANDELSON
IRIS BARRY
GWENDOLYN BENNETT
ADELAIDE CRAPSEY
MARY CAROLYN DAVIES
HILDA DOOLITTLE
HILDEGARDE FLANNER
F.S. FLINT
JUN FUJITA
SADAKICHI HARTMANN
T.E. HULME
TAKEKO KUJO
AMY LOWELL
MINA LOY
YONE NOGUCHI
CHARLES REZNIKOFF
EDWARD STORER
MARIE TUDOR-GARLAND
AKIKO YOSHINO
AKIKO YANAGIWARA
& MANY MORE

FORGOTTENPOETS.COM

BLAST

No. 2. July, 1915.

*"Good art is concerned with the making of gods or of toys—
creations of almost equivalent power."*

—Jessie Dismorr (1919)

MONOLOGUE.

My niche in nonentity still grins—
I lay knees, elbows pinioned, my sleep mutterings
    blunted against a wall.

Pushing my hard head through the hole of birth
    I squeezed out with intact body.
I ache all over, but acrobatic, I undertake
    the feat of existence.
Details of equipment delight me.

I admire my arrogant spiked tresses, the disposition
    of my perpetually foreshortened limbs,
Also the new machinery that wields the chains of
    muscles fitted beneath my close coat of skin.

On a pivot of contentment my balanced body
        moves slowly.
Inquisitiveness, a butterfly, escapes.
It spins with drunken invitation. I poke my fingers
        into the middles of big succulent flowers.
My fingers are fortunately tipped with horn.

Tentacles of my senses, subtle and far-reaching,
    drop spoils into the vast sack of my greed.
Stretched ears projecting from my brain are gongs
    struck by vigorous and brutal fists of air.

Into scooped nets of nostrils glide slippery and
    salt scents, I swallow slowly with gasps.
In pursuit of shapes my eyes dilate and bulge.
Finest instruments of touch they refuse to blink
    their pressure of objects.

They dismember live anatomies innocently.
They run around the polished rims of rivers.
With risk they press against the cut edges
    of rooks and pricking pinnacles.

Pampered appetites and curiosities become
    blood-drops, their hot mouths yell war.
Sick opponents dodging behind silence,
    echo alone shrills an equivalent threat.
Obsessions rear their heads. I hammer
    their faces into discs.
Striped malignities spring upon me,
    and tattoo with incisions of wild claws.

Speeded with whips of hurt, I hurry towards
　　　ultimate success.
I stoop to link the bright cups of pain and
　　　drop out of activity.

I lie a slack bag of skin. My nose hangs over
the abyss of exhaustion, my loosened tongue
　　　laps sleep as from a bowl of milk.

LONDON NOTES.

[selections]

I. IN PARK LANE.

Long necked feminine structures support
almost without grimacing the elegant
discomfort of restricted elbows.

II. HYDE PARK.

Commonplace, titanic figures with a splendid
motion stride across the parched plateau of grass,
little London houses only a foot high
huddle at their heels.

Under trees all the morning women sit sewing
and knitting, their monotonous occupation
accompanying the agreeable muddle
of their thoughts.

In the Row. Vitality civilized to a needles-point;
highly-bred men and horses pass swiftly in useless
delightful motion; women walk enamoured of
their own accomplished movements.

III. BRITISH MUSEUM.

Gigantic cubes of iron rock are set in a
    parallelogram of orange sand.
Ranks of black columns of immense weight
and immobility are threaded by a stream
    of angular volatile shapes.
Their trunks shrink quickly in retreat
    towards the cavernous roof.
Innumerable pigeons fret the stone steps
    with delicate restlessness.

IV. READING-ROOM.

This colossal globe of achievement presses upon
two-hundred cosmopolitan foreheads,
    respectfully inclined.

V. PICCADILLY.

The embankment of brick and stone is fancifully
    devised and stuck with flowers and flags.
Towers of scaffolding draw their criss-cross pattern
    of bars upon the sky, a monstrous tartan.
Delicate fingers of cranes describe beneficent
    motions in space.
Glazed cases contain curious human specimens.
Nature with a brush of green pigment paints rural
    landscape up to the edge of the frame.
Pseudo-romantic hollows and hillocks are peopled
    by reality prostrate and hostile.

VI. FLEET STREET

Precious slips of houses, packed like books
on a shelf, are littered all over with signs
    and letters.
A dark, agitated stream straggles turbulently
along the channel bottom;
    clouds race overhead.
Curiously exciting are so many perspective
lines, withdrawing, converging;
they indicate evidently
    something of importance
        beyond the limits of sight.

PROMENADE.

With other delicate and malicious children,
a horde bright-eyed with bodies easily tired,
I follow Curiosity, the reticent and maidenly
governess of our adoration.

I am surprised to observe, in a converging
        thoroughfare, Hunger the vulgar usher,
whipping up his tribe of schoolboys, who,
questing hither and thither on robust limbs,
        fill the air with loud and innocent cries.

The suspicion suddenly quickens within me
that there is an understanding. It is possible
that we are being led by different ways into
        the same prohibited
                and doubtful neighbourhood.

PAYMENT.

Now that money is passing between us, for that
which has no equivalent in coin, I will give
you a shilling for your peculiar smile, and
sixpence for the silken sweep of your dress;
and for your presence, the strange thing that
    I can neither grasp nor elude,
        I will give you another shilling.

MATILDA.

Strange that a beauty so dangerously near
perfection should choose life without
    happenings and hedged in completely
By habits and hand-labours

Set in an ordered and commonplace rightness.
It is certain that she has no sense of play at all,
Coveting neither delight nor risk, nor the uses
    of her supreme gift:
So that within a homespun sobriety
The dread thing passes unperceived
    by most comers,
And chiefly secure from self-recognition
By strait bonds of chastity and duties
    ardently cherished.

POEMS 1918

"The Stars are threshed, and the
Souls are threshed from their husks."
—William Blake

RHAPSODY.

They escape into strong sun-light, the indignant
and impassioned children, springing from
caresses,
     their skin revolted at the touch of hands.

With stern eyes dissecting maternal ardours they
surprise therein the chemistry of re-absorption.
     (It is the inadmissible experiment.)

Shall they yield lips to that fluid, whose action
must dissolve the shapeliness of their fine entities?
     Whence shall they extract life?

Swiftness feeds them, pressure of flying dust,
     the ceaseless dislodgement of space.

They break into calls one to another, more
        radiant than song.
Each call is the ignition of a new dawn.
Nothing responds to them on earth. It is
become a desert whose amazed stare
        allows them passage.
What equivalent could it offer in tree or flood?
The indignity of its routine, its wobbling circuit—
        how the finality of its course shames
                their divagations!

No possible halt nor error! Their way is a clear
sword upon which melancholy has not breathed.
They are not accessible to pain or loss:
    their sapience can dispense with measure.

The droppings of their flying thought are
star-dust fallen through the dark.

MATINÉE.

The Croisette trembles in the violent
    matutinal light.
Shapes quicken and pass: the day moves.
My nerves spring to their task of
    acquisitiveness.

The secret of my success is a knowledge
    of the limitedness of time.
Economy is scientific: I understand the
    best outlay of attention.

Within this crazy shell an efficient
    machinery mints satisfactions.

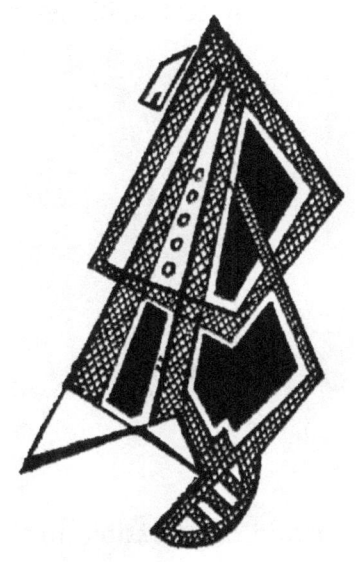

Your pity is a systematic mistake. I may yet grow
arrogant on the wastage of other lives.
　　The holes of my sack spill treasure.

Who but I should be accessible to the naked
　　pressure of things?
Between me and apprehension no passions draw
　　their provoking dissimulative folds.

I have not clouded heaven with the incense
    of personal demand.
Myself and the universe are two entities.
Those unique terms admit the possibility
    of clean intercourse.

All liaisons smell of an inferior social grade;
    but alliance can dispense with fusion and touch
I treat with respect the sparkling and gesticulating
dust that confronts me: of it are compounded
fruits and diamonds, superb adolescents,
    fine manners.

This pigment disposed by the ultimate vibrations
of force paints the universe in a
contemporary mode.

I am glad that it is up-to-date and ephemeral,
that I am to be diverted
by a succession of fantasies.

The static cannot claim my approval. I live
in the act of departure. Eternity is for those
    who can dispose of an amplitude of time.

Pattern is enough. I pray you do not
    mention the soul.
Give me detail, and the ardent ceremonial of
    commonplaces that means nothing.

Oh, the ennui of inconceivable space!
My traveling spirit will taste too soon
    of emptiness.
I thrill to the microscopic. I plunder the
    close-packed cells
        and burrows of life.
The local has always the richness
    of a brocade:
        it is worth while to explore
        the design.

I spell happiness out of dots and dashes;
    a ray, a tone, the insignificance
      of a dangling leaf.
Provided it have a factual existence the least
    atom will suffice my need.
But I cannot stomach shadows.
    It is certain that the physical
      round world would fit my mouth
        like a lollipop.

You ask: To what end this petty and ephemeral
busyness, this last push of human sensation?
Is one then a neophyte in philosophy,
    demanding reasons and results?

I proclaim life to the end a piece of artistry,
    essentially idle and exquisite.
The trinkets stored within my coffin
    will outlast my dust.

EVENT.

I was the top-most apple on the tree.
A blossom has fruited beyond me.

Whereas it was casualness I cultivated
And a dainty indifference to credit,
It shall now be Faith, Hope & Charity,
A code of common notices
And the stooping grace.

Else must I split with my spite
    And not among sodden roots!

THE PRESENT.

Oh, actuality,
Into thy rare flood
Where meet all waters
I plunge this body
With contentment!

Slowly we learn the taste of happiness.
With what travail of brain-cells
And a rigorous aesthetic
Ensues the connection
Of the necessity of this joy.

Yet the spinning liquid
That laves me
Is surely the solution
Of a million coloured gems!

INTERROGATION.

The just mood spent fulminating
Against the soiled intricacies
Of a sweetish civilization,
Betakes its anger
To a plot of solitude,
There against encroachment
To strengthen the granite
Of a contemptuous peace.

· · · · ·

Is this then, oh honour,
The sum of all interrogation?
A clean withdrawal,
And power inexperimented
    In too slight material?

    A security
Issueless, impermeable,
Close simulacre of the sheet pocket of death?

Think you with such immaculacy
To blunt the general urge,
Or punish the push of atoms
And obstinate burgeoning
    In cracks of mortar?

Dare you, oh honesty complete,
    Blink the eventuality
        Of a toppled defense?

Or could it be rather
An original prudency
That this averted aspect,
Contesting no sweep of the central impulses
And one with life's business,
Presents the mode of an exigent masculinity
Sifting earth for its mate?

PRELUDE.

This is the desired moment. Now activities crowd
upon me. Initiations twist themselves into the
shapes of words.

My impulse stirs the fragments of which
    earth is composed:
there is a movement towards the classic
    and complete.

I call the universe to order. The irregularity of
phenomena is no longer supportable.

These individuals must surrender their
angularities of character and fit themselves
with complacency into the shape of music.

Life and experience organize a last rebellion.
There is a juggling of atoms, a sudden
gymnastic of force.

My antagonists, you are my predestined material!
     These are the pieces of my game:
Dreams, the very flow of facts, hereditary thirsts
stringing varied existences upon a thread of care,
Keen, trembling hates, weapons with sure points
that prick invisibility, nostalgias whose veins are
     flooded with too rich a dye,
And those, the final flashes, snapt short and
     sputtering in ruin, and the stench
          that fills up the dark.

Personalities long inviolate, you are appointed
instruments without degradation.
(For in secret for ages the immaculate republic
sought a tyrant to be the recipient of its tears.)

Resistance is the climax of your beauty.
Your moment of perfection is alone
    serviceable.

What metamorphosis awaits beyond the
    limits of surrender?
You shall be driven into what cold moulds
    of perfected form?

MAIDEN'S PRAYER.

The thought comes "Shall I be happy?"
    and with the doubt
Trembles my flowery trellis, the bright
    streamers are pushed aside.

Sweet Nature, I run to you to hold me
    till this fright is past.
If I am not fortunate I am nothing.
    I cannot scheme conquest.

But you are my Mother; your management
    shall supplement my small wits.
I prepared my filial kiss night and morning;
my white prayers flew against your bosom
    in mistake for God.

(Alas, He scares me, the strange one.
    His eye is neither male nor female.)

But you have no trace of Justice. Your stoop
  is toward the well favoured.
When I touch my bosom in supplication I
  grow confident.

Oh, I am docile and tender. I have observed
  you and moulded myself.
I heel and toe to your pulses. I waver to the
  stream of your breath.
I am but one of your children and not
  mutinous.

The grass waves, the moth flutters and I dance.
La, la, la, this folly! You Mother will not
  mistake it for idleness.
I turn with a click of my delicate heels,
  unminding the vast reverberations in space.
I am too well bred to listen, to stare or to
  ask questions.

The song might drown on my lips and
    the spinning world drop slack.
But the danger was prepared for—my
    nature prohibits recognizance.

My shallowness threads the generations,
    and the silk will hold.
All wisdom is barren, you have said it,
    the last state before death.
I hold the creed. Make me fortunate!

For I admit nothing, oh Mother,
save the tinkling of tunes
that run in my blood
And each fancy that starts a faint
physical pulse, and ends
in a cascade of flowers.

CELIA.

She has preferred energy to beauty,
    friendship to love,
to children a dozen secular activities.

Thus is prolonged the youth of her fine
    body and all its swiftness.

The sorrows she has encountered are not
the sorrows of her sex, they are owned
    without confusion.

Delightful is her laughter, the chime of
    true appreciations.
Clear her tones, free from malice.
How fairly toward life she lifts an
    unchastened eye-lid!

But her courage is a flaw of the intelligence.
The Past and the Future deal idly with her:
she is a spend-thrift of her hour.

She has not on several occasions seen death
draw close swollen through the medium of fear.
She remains unbaptized to this date.

THE
LITTLE REVIEW

VOL. VI.   AUGUST, 1919   No. 4

"The mess and muddle of an artist's personal life is the chaos from which evolves the order of creation."

—Jessie Dismorr (1919)

Spring

The excessive sweetness of bird's singing pierces
the thin epidermis of inattentive thought.

Pale poison, it creeps along the channels
of the nerves, thrills in the finger tips,
    becomes diffused in the blood.
Because of it all appetite for appearances
turns to nausea; the senses reject their diet
    of accustomed joys.

Only essential seems that singular stabbing
of edged notes, irregular, mercilessly
    unsubdued to music.

The Enemy

The microbe that inhabits my body makes
me sick; but it is he that pushes me to
impossible and exasperated feats of skill.
He drinks my strength, then pushes me to
unwilling exploration.

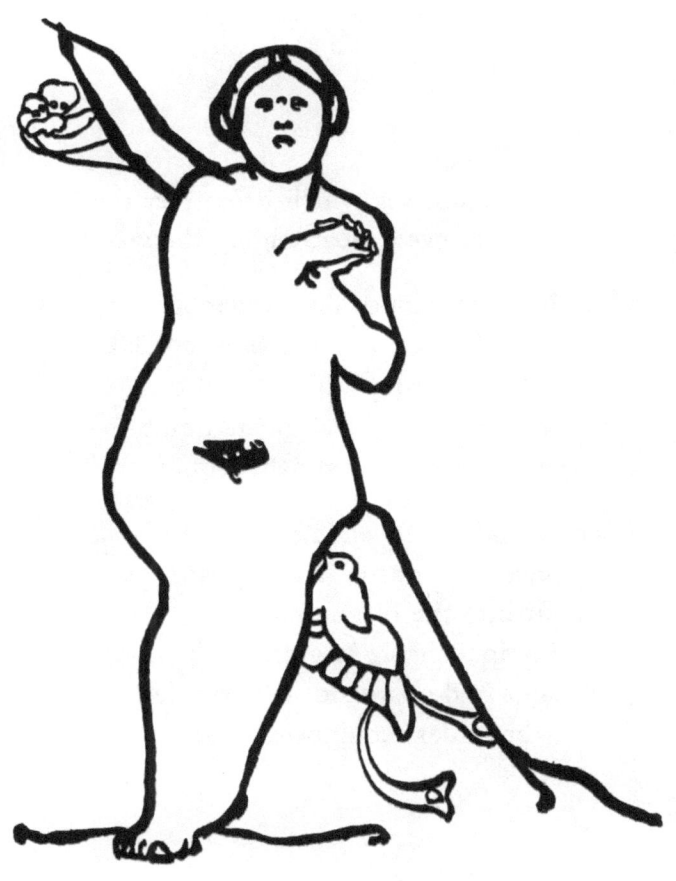

Islands

In that restless sea which is eternity the little
islands of event float among the waves.

(Are they water blossoms with roots
continually shaken, floating their petals
    on the pulsating water?
Are they a flotilla of frail boats trembling
to the touches of interminable ripples?)

Even at flood time when from some ocean
of inconceivable vastness the great tides
    pour into the brimming sea,
    the imperishable islands,
    fragile and obstinate, achieve their
        breathless equilibrium.

Twilight

Erect and of a curious emaciation the tall
virgin paces the sands at nightfall.
Around her limbs the wind twists her sinuous
garments, the locks are whirled
about her bossy temples.

The treasure within her bosom is the finely
    selected material that fits into a little space.
The talisman is discreet but absolute.
She is immune from dissolution forever.
    (Oh Sorrow, Oh Penalty,
        Life has eluded her contact).

The pain that is her heart, the swiftness of her
    limbs, these are the last gift of civilization.
But her arbitrary erectness is eternally menaced.
Sea and sand and the bars of sinking cloud
    do not cease to urge her to the level
        of Nature's indiscriminate embrace.

Promenade

With other delicate and malicious children,
    a horde bright eyed whose bodies
easily tire, I follow Curiosity, the refined and
    maidenly governess of our adoration.

I am surprised to notice in an emerging
    thoroughfare Hunger, the vulgar usher,
    whipping up his tribe of schoolboys,
    who, questing hither and thither on robust
    limbs, fill the air with loud
        and innocent cries.

The suspicion quickens within me that
    there is an understanding.
We are being led by different ways
    into the same doubtful
        and prohibited neighborhood.

Landscape

The immense gray sky, wheeling towards me
and on to me, against it I have—what resource?
In the swarthy limbs of the trees that march over
me as I lie pallid, holding to the earth, what danger!
Nevertheless a creature thus drugged and bound
by immortality, am I not already destroyed
by the rigorous onrush of time?

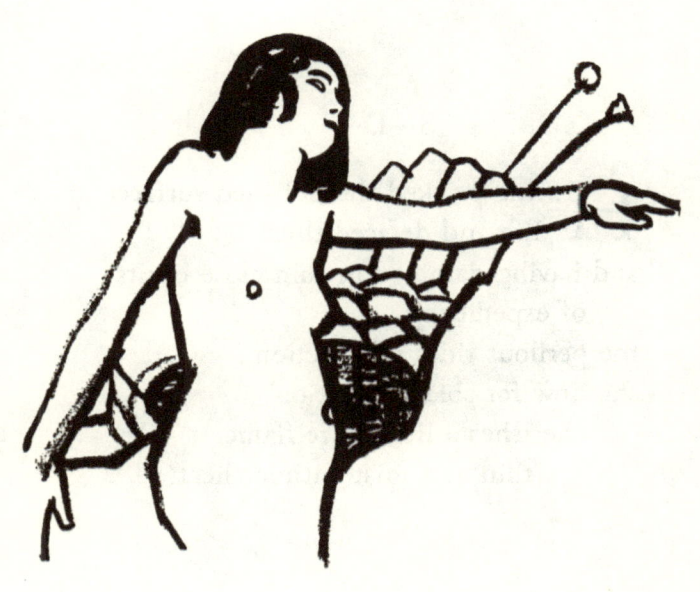

Having pricked the polished surfaces of
life and defaced them
and having dammed in thin close limits
of expediency
the perilous tides of affection
she now for sole occupation
cherishes a little pure flame,
thin as a mist without heat.

> *This Space for Your
> Thoughts*

THE OLD EXPRESSIONS ARE WITH US ALWAYS
AND THERE ARE ALWAYS OTHERS

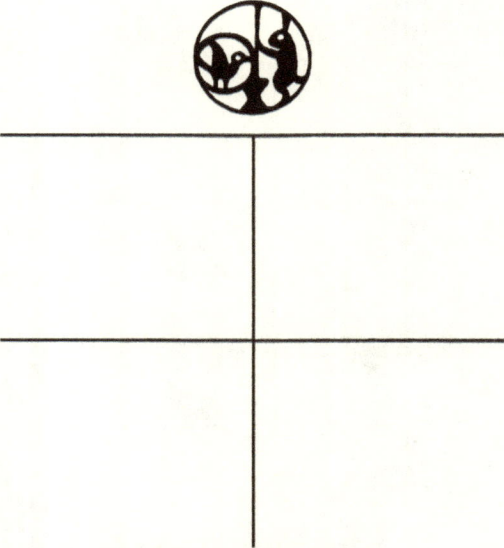

Please handle with care.

www.ingramcontent.com/pod-product-compliance
Lightning Source LLC
Chambersburg PA
CBHW031448120626
46545CB00006B/2605